STEAM MEMORIES: 1950

No.19: NORTH EAST SCRAPYARDS

Including: Clayton & Davie; Ellis Metals; Hughes, Bolckows;
W. Willoughby & Darlington Works

ISBN 1-899624-98-0

INTRODUCTION

The gradual demise of steam throughout the late 1960s was a closely followed process, catching the attention of both enthusiasts and, to some extent, the general public. To the casual spectator the move from steam to diesel signified another progressive step towards new technologies and the future, but to those whose imagination had been caught and carried by the age of steam this was a time of great sadness and immense loss.

Scrapyards, the length and breadth of the country became the last vestige of steam, a place of passing over, where photographers both curious and respectful would gather to document the end of an era. The scrapyards of the North East were rich in wares; Darlington scrapyard in particular cut up the majority of locomotives that had been maintained in the nearby works, encompassing a considerable number of different classes. Clayton & Davie on the banks of the Tyne at Dunston, Ellis Metals in nearby Swalwell and Hughes, Bolckows and Willoughbys, both in south-east Northumberland, were much smaller private yards by comparison, serving to take over the work of Darlington at its closure in 1964.

This album serves to give an insight into all of the aforementioned scrapyards as seen through the lenses of Ian Falcus, Howard Forster, Dave Tyreman, Trevor Ermel, Ian Spencer, the late Walter Hodgson and Eric Wilson, all of whom dedicated their time and patience to the documentation of many a locomotive in its final hours.

With special thanks to Alan Brooks and Eric Colling for the use of their collections in addition to those named above.

David Dunn, Cramlington. September 2008

(previous page) With enthusiasts young and old making their way around the carnage at North Road, a one-time Boston allocated K2 No.61757, stands forlorn at the entrance of the scrapyard on 15th March 1959. Cutting is well advanced with the footplate, rods and cab already dealt with. Note the smokebox numberplate still intact although the shedplate has been removed (probably at Boston before the engine left). This was one of seven members of the class to suffer a similar fate at Darlington. *I.Falcus*.

Printed and bound by The Amadeus Press, Cleckheaton, West Yorkshire
First published in the United Kingdom by Book Law Publications, 382 Carlton Hill, Nottingham, NG4 1JA

DARLINGTON NORTH ROAD LOCOMOTIVE WORKS

The scrap yard on North Road Darlington had few equals for variety, quantity and quality. Since 1948 the dedicated scrapyard at North Road and the Stripping shop within the main works managed to demolish, cut up, dismantle and scrap into oblivion more than 1,600 steam locomotives - thats an average of two every week from 1st January 1948 to closure of the scrapyard in 1964. Of course, it did not quite work like that because some weeks there may not have been any customers - the pictures hereafter tell their own story - but on other weeks the scrapping became manic and sometimes two engines a day were obliterated. The number of different classes dealt with is extremely interesting and virtually every former LNER class which worked during the British Railways era was represented in the Darlington list of casualties. But, not only was the LNER represented, the London Midland & Scottish Railway produced a fair number of designs which met their end at North Road. Add to them the BR Standard classes, along with the two types of WD tender engines, and we have a mix to rival any single location in the country.

Below is presented a list of the numerous classes 'handled' at the scrapyard with the approximate number of engines from that class actually dealt with. The list does not appertain to be 100% accurate and is really a representation of the numbers put through. Individual locomotive numbers are not included because space does not allow. However, digest the list and ponder on the amount of metal recycled and of the chances lost in saving a specific class, especially towards the end when, for three grand, you could purchase a working Pacific. You could also buy a nice detached house on the edge of town or about a dozen Ford Anglias!

DARLINGTON BR Locomotive Works Scrapping List since 1948:

A1 - 2; A3 - 9; A4 - 2; A5 - 42; A6 - 9; A7 - 20; A8 - 45
B1 - 54; B7 - 2; B16 - 55.
C1 - 9; C6 - 4; C7 - 14; C13 - 2.
D1 - 1; D9 - 3; D20 - 49; D49 - 73.
F3 - 2.
G5 - 107.
J10 - 9; J11 - 1; J15 - 2; J21 - 70; J24 - 31; J25 - 74; J26 - 50; J27 - 45; J39 - 22; J63 - 3;
J65 - 1; J69 - 1; J71 - 76; J72 - 89; J73 - 10; J75 - 1; J77 - 42; J93 - 2; J94 - 46.
K1 - 1; K2 - 7.
L1 - 85; L3 - 1.
N4 - 1; N5 - 21; N8 - 30; N9 - 19; N10 - 19; N13 - 10.
O4 - 1.
Q1 - 5; Q4 - 6; Q5 - 76; Q6 - 49; Q7 - 14.
S1 - 5.
T1 - 13.
V1/V3 - 64; V2 - 45.
Y1 - 17; Y3 - 7; Y8 - 2.
BR Cl.6 'Clan' - 5; BR Cl.2 - 1.
WD 2-8-0 - 48; WD 2-10-0 - 12.
LMS Stanier Cl3 2-6-2T - 6; Ivatt Cl.2 2-6-2T - 2; Cl4 2-6-4T- 3; Cl.4 2-6-0 'Crab' - 3; Cl.4 Ivatt - 2; 4F 0-6-0 - 15;
LMS Stanier Cl.5 4-6-0 - 1; 'Jubilee' 4-6-0 - 2; Ivatt Cl.2 - 12; 3F 0-6-0T - 4; 8F 2-8-0 - 5.

Nearing its demise on 2nd March 1957, was former Malton based G5 No.67346, which is still carrying all of its cast iron plates. The whistle positioned on the roof was a very unusual feature on a British Railways period G5. *I.Falcus*.

Just arrived from Selby shed on 12th June 1954, was D20 No.62392 fitted with a flush sided tender. I remember reading in the Railway Observer that some D20s were being fitted with J39 type tenders. These were actually NE coal rail tenders with the coal rails removed, and a full plated skin fitted over the top, giving the impression of a Group Standard tender. The clues are a just behind the cab, you can see the double skin at the front of the tender and also the NER axleboxes and springs. This class ended their days working the Alnmouth to Alnwick and Alnmouth to Newcastle local trains. *I.Falcus.*

Little and Large. Sent from Hull Springhead, A7 No.69787 stands awaiting its fate adjacent to an equally filthy J71 on 5th September 1954. Two stacks of redundant wheel tyres lie beside the locomotive. The semi-botanical setting of the scrapyard seems somewhat surreal. *I.Falcus.*

In the scrapyard during September 1961, and in an almost impossible position to escape trapped between a condemned L1 and B16, was Departmental Locomotive No 54, formerly Y1 No.68153, which had worked the yard at the Darlington Permanent Way depot for the whole of its life. Although it too was withdrawn, it was subsequently reprieved and sold to the Middleton Railway at Leeds with a low mileage guarantee. The tiny engine has even got a lamp showing in anticipation of its forthcoming release. *I.Falcus.*

D49/2 'Hunt' No.62727 THE QUORN inside the graveyard on 4th March 1961. This 4-4-0 was fitted with a Great Central type 'B' tender having give up its Group Standard tender to a new V2 class engine in 1942. Altogether twenty-eight D49 lost their GS tenders in favour of the GC type but later ten of the GC tenders were given completely new bodies, similar to the GS body, on the original GC chassis. So how did we tell the difference - look at the valence - on the GC tender it is twice the depth of that on the locomotive, this was an easy way of identifying a flush sided tender which had GC origins. Note that the fox is missing from the nameplate - they were easily removed! But what of the nameplate? *I.Falcus.*

The sad remains of the first B16/1 to be withdrawn, No.61474, is well on its way to oblivion, being viewed by a probable modeller on the 16th March 1958. Look at all the detail on show; footplate brackets, cylinders and steam manifold. To the left is the front end of an A8 looking destined to a similar fate. *I.Falcus.*

The last D20 No.62395, withdrawn in November 1957, lies in the scrapyard looking splendid indeed on 12th January 1958. Wanted by enthusiasts for preservation, British Railways refused the request because there was a NER 4-4-0 already preserved; however they agreed to paint it on one side only for an official photograph, what a shame! As a small boy, aged 12 years, I had walked through the scrapyard taking numbers and thought it odd that an ex works engine was in the place. *I.Falcus*.

On the same January day in 1958, an extremely large T1, No.69913, recently withdrawn from Newport Middlesbrough, stands alongside G5 No.67259 awaiting the cutters torch. ***I.Falcus.***

Push-pull fitted G5 No.67261 was allocated to South Blyth at the formation of British Railways, and then transferred to Botanic Gardens shed in Hull on 21st November 1954. Here in the scrapyard on 26th May 1957, it was presumably condemned. It was then rescued and taken to Gateshead works for a General overall, repainted and had the later BR crest affixed. Afterwards the G5 transferred back to South Blyth shed, to operate push-pull services on the Monkseaton-Blyth-Newbiggin lines. On the 26th October 1958 it did a short hop to 'Mackemland' running the last month of its life on the South Shields-Sunderland push-pull service before making the final journey to the scrapyard in December 1958. Mistakes did sometimes happen, albeit very rarely, when a locomotive was sent prematurely to the scrapyard but in the case of this G5 it was more a matter of requiring its services because nothing else was available. The train of boilers was either en route back to the main workshops, where the boilers could be refurbished for further use, or perhaps they were off to Gateshead with the G5 running mid-train. The final theory being that they could have been purchased by a scrap dealer, even at this early date BR had started to sell redundant boilers to the private yards. *I.Falcus.*

The sole occupant in the scrapyard on Sunday 29th April 1956 was a Westinghouse fitted, Sunderland based G5 No.67347. Condemned a month earlier, the 0-4-4T would soon be cut up and loaded into four or five mineral wagons and taken away. A party of enthusiasts compare notes whilst to their left, and parked up for the weekend, is a well loaded British Road Services 8-wheel Leyland Octopus. The throughput of this scrapyard was prodigious and although some enthusiasts visited monthly, it required more frequent visits than that to keep up with the comings and the goings. *I.Falcus.*

It is 29th May 1960 and the onset of diesel multiple units during 1957/58 sounded the death knell for many tank engines, large or small, and as a result redundant A8s Nos.69874 and 69875 await their fate at Darlington. This view was captured from virtually the same spot as the previous illustration albeit from a lower elevation but note how the trees have grown since 1956. *I.Falcus.*

Going right back in time now to 19th May 1951 and we have a very early shot of NER electric locomotive No.26504 with D20 No.62353 for company. The electric was due to go to Sheffield with the rest of the class for scrapping at a private yard but its bogies were needed as spares for No.26510 at Ilford. The latter electric became Departmental No.100. The combination of North Eastern lettering, together with a British Railways number is most unusual if not unique. *E.Wilson.*

Ex LMS 4F No.43942 of Royston shed, Thompson B1 No.61288 of York and a pair of J94s await their fate on a murky 31st January 1964. By now the yard was going all out to eliminate as many locomotives as possible because closure was not too far away. However, throughout 1964 former LMS engines resident at the North Eastern Region sheds in Yorkshire began to appear in large numbers at Darlington for scrapping. The 4F had been condemned on shed in December but instead of the usual long period being dumped at the back of the shed it was sent to Darlington post haste. Further down the yard, behind the photographer, lay a couple more 4Fs and an Ivatt Cl.2MT No.41273 from Farnley Junction. *D.Tyreman.*

More Gresley D49s but these are Part 1 engines. No.62711 DUMBARTONSHIRE, ex St Margarets, dozing in the company of No.62718 KINROSS-SHIRE; down the yard was No.62716 KINCARDINESHIRE. All three still carried nameplates, worksplates and smokebox number plates but not shed plates. The date - 16th April 1961. Who removed the plates before the scrapping started and where did all that precious metalwork go? One particular V2 nameplate (see the Darlington album in this series) ended up as a boot scraper at the nearby locomotive workshops, covered in mud! Note that No.62711 was coupled to a rebuilt GC flush sided tender. *H.Forster.*

Taken out of service on the 19th August 1957 after seventy-eight years of toil, J77 No.68426, graces the scrapyard with its presence on 1st September. A real old-timer, this engine came from North Blyth shed where it was used to push coal wagons onto the staithes at its home port. Rebuilt in 1904 to 0-6-0T configuration, the tank was sent to North Blyth to help the export drive. In 1938, with war looming and coal exports drastically being curtailed, the J77 was transferred to Blaydon but towards the end of hostilities when coastal colliers could ship coal to the Thames in relative safety, the 0-6-0T was sent back to Blyth to once again bark its way up the slopes of the staithes with loaded hoppers. To the left of the engine, outside the scrapyard, the long gone British Road Services office based in North Road station can be seen - this is now Darlington Railway Museum. Note the fairly new 16T mineral wagon which was about to be bashed about somewhat with a load of scrap metal. ***H.Forster.***

A wonderfully detailed shot of a pair of V3 boilers in November 1963, showing tubes, front plate, superheater elements and firebox stays. The intricacy of the workings are akin to a pipe organ or a music box. Note the abandoned, upturned stool presumably left by a cutter, on a 'bait-break' perhaps? ***W.P.Hodgson.***

One for the ladies! A rich hiding ground in November 1963 for these two tabby kittens amongst the grounded boilers. Visible are a V3 and a B1 boiler. Note the electric light box on the top of the B1 smokebox and the brackets on the V3 smokebox front for the North British area destination boards, also the fine scale hand rail knobs. ***W.P.Hodgson*****.**

In late 1956 Darlington undertook the overflow of withdrawn engines destined to be cut up at Gorton . These were denoted by a white cross for withdrawal but this engine was never part of the ritual having been in store at Doncaster. Here can be seen S1 0-8-4T No.69901 on 9th February 1957, languishing in the scrap yard with sections of the footplate and hand rails removed. Note the layers of the British Railways decal and the earlier lettering showing through the weathered paintwork, illustrating the timeline of liveries of this particular locomotive. Still intact is what would now be the highly desirable smokebox number plate (Oh to own it now!). The unusual rear bogie had previously been fitted with a booster to increase the tractive effort needed to hump shunt trains at Wath marshalling yard. ***H.Forster.***

(above) The sombre signs of Gorton's white cross denoting the imminent withdrawal of N5 No.69250, ironically a Gorton allocated engine. This was the scrap yard on Saturday 6th October 1956 when the Gorton overflow became more than a trickle. (below) On the same day a depressed looking, chalked up C13 No.67425, also from the Gorton stud, graces the yard with its elegant lines. It is a shame that its only visit to this area was for cutting up. *both H.Forster.*

An unusual coach can be seen lurking in the right background beside two withdrawn D20s, Nos.62372 and 62378. Bereft of tenders, they look somewhat anaemic in the cold winter light of 10th November 1956. The former engine had been condemned on Bonfire Night with the latter engine receiving its verdict next day. Both engines were fifty years old so had repaid their initial investment handsomely. *H.Forster.*

A push-pull fitted G5, No.67282, formerly of Hull Botanic Gardens shed, nestled between sister engine No.67273, and a withdrawn boiler stripped down to bare tubes. The date is 12th May 1957 and the scrap yard is working flat out to clear a back log of withdrawn North Eastern engines which have started to mount up at the works. Both of these locomotives were fitted with high hoppers on their coal bunkers. On close inspection this image reveals breather pipes on the cab roof, one in each corner, which allowed the air to remain at constant pressure above the water in the tanks. ***H.Forster.***

Mid-week 'working' shots at the scrapyard were not common. This one shows a boiler being raised through the trackside scrub in October 1963. Rather poignantly the buildings on the left-hand side are the Hopetown workshops of the erstwhile Stockton & Darlington Railway, where the new Peppercorn A1 No.60163 TORNADO had been built recently, overlooking the graveyard of many of it's ancestors. ***W.P.Hodgson.***

A view of the backheads of two derelict boilers showing the double handed Gresley regulators, designed so that the locomotive could be driven from either side. Interestingly, on preserved Gresley engines, the right hand side handle has been removed to prevent the fireman from being hit when the driver opened the regulator. The fate of these two boilers is chalked on their flanks and the steam crane seen working hard in the left background may not have to move them again - at least in one piece. ***W.P.Hodgson.***

A superb shot of an unidentified B16 backhead albeit bereft of fittings. The October 1963 photograph shows the position of reverser, vacuum ejector, cab doors, seats and firebox door. In close company alongside are J72 No.69004 and J50 No.68892. ***W.P.Hodgson.***

BR Standard Class 6 Pacific No.72001 CLAN CAMERON awaiting entry to the scrapyard in November 1963. A good view of the external pipework on these standard locomotives. A key feature in the design of the BR Standard Pacifics was easy access for maintenance, which resulted in much of this outside plumbing and regulator linkage. The complexity of the external bits has become a nightmare for railway modellers. Apparently the 'Clans' were never a favourite of the Scottish drivers - they were reputed to use too much coal and water - but they did look pretty good. Note that by now the nameplates had been removed long before this one and only visit to Darlington. In front of the Pacific is one of the WD 2-10-0s which arrived from the Scottish Region at the same time as the 'Clans' and caused much excitement, and a certain amount of surprise, amongst the visiting enthusiasts. ***W.P.Hodgson.***

Looking like something on the modelling bench, these are skeletal frames of BR Clan No.72004 CLAN MACDONALD in October 1963. This was the first of the five 'Clans' (Nos.72000 to 72004) to be dispatched at Darlington. ***W.P.Hodgson.***

This image encapsulates the pathos of the scrapyard showing a scattering of locomotive parts strewn by the tracks in November 1963. In the foreground is the bunker of T1 4-8-0T No.69921, the last engine to be built at Gateshead works and cut up here in July 1961. It appears to have been untidily left to slowly deteriorate but on closer inspection it looks as though it could have been used as a coal store and may explain why it was still present two years after it's withdrawal. North Road scrapyard kept a number of 'bits' such as the two Sentinel bodies used for stores and break cabins. It was a wonderful place to visit and explore. It was steeped in railway history and it had become one of the premier BR scrapyards during its final years of operation. *W.P.Hodgson.*

BR Darlington built J72 No.69004 on Saturday 19th October 1963. A one time local engine, the 0-6-0T had started its working life at Darlington shed in November 1949, thereafter transferring to Thornaby in August 1961, back to 51A in February 1962 and then Gateshead a month later. Nearly fourteen years on from leaving the main erecting shop at Darlington for the first time, it has come back and is now at its final resting place. Note the high hopper of the ex Great Northern J50 buffered up at the far left of the image. ***W.P.Hodgson.***

J50 No.68935, ex Ardsley in November 1963, nose to nose with a partially stripped down Q6 boiler, showing the honeycombed remains of the asbestos lagging open to the elements, with not a Health & Safety inspector in sight. ***W.P.Hodgson.***

Clayton & Davie (Shipbreakers and Metal Merchants) Dunston on Tyne

Not far from the Ellis Metals yard at Swalwell, the Clayton & Davie yard clung to the south bank of the Tyne at Dunston, opposite Elswick on the north bank. The yard's origins go back to ship breaking besides general scrap merchants and it was well placed, when the time came, to accept condemned BR locomotives from the nearby goods lines which skirted the property. The numbers of engines dealt with at this yard were modest and most had been sourced locally with one or two decent 'foreigners' thrown in for good measure.

CLAYTON & DAVIE Scrapping List:

LMS Ivatt Cl.4 2-6-0	43000	43015	43050	43055	43063	43070	43117	43123	43137
LMS Cl.4F 0-6-0	44367								
LMS 'Jubilee 4-6-0	45573	45608							
LNER Peppercorn A1 4-6-2	60117	60133	60156						
LNER Gresley V2 2-6-2	60876	60886	60946						
LNER Q6 0-8-0	63346	63407	63413	63420	63429	63431	63440	63458	
LNER J27 0-6-0	65792	65833	65892						
BR Standard 9F 2-10-0	92167								

An historically rich panorama of Clayton & Davie's yard in September 1967, encompassing the changing skyline of the Elswick district of Newcastle. In the distance a crane can be seen erecting typically 1960s high-rise flats (no mention of T.Dan Smith please) above the turn of the century row upon row of terraced housing that dominate the landscape below. Also barely visible 'nosing out' to the left, behind the yard office, is a steam ship which was a regular sight beside the Vickers-Armstrong's works. Apart from the aforementioned block of flats and the river, everything else in this photograph has been redeveloped. Now to the engines in the yard which were front right to left: J27 No.65833, Q6 No.63346, Ivatt 4MT No.43055, Q6s Nos.63429 and 63431, with Ivatt 4MT No.43123 bringing up the rear. To the extreme left, hiding behind the yard cranes, can be seen one of the more usual occupants of the wharf here - a dredger. ***T.Ermel.***

A line of withdrawn tenders stand on the bank of the Tyne, 31st August 1967. The collection included those from a V2, J27, Q6, C6 ex NE Atlantic and a couple from Ivatt Class 4MTs. Hiding is a Q6 the chimney of which can be seen above the tender on the right. One may wonder why these tenders have been spared thus far? Well, apparently such vehicles had further uses at large industrial installations such as steel works, chemical plants, coking plants (same thing) or anywhere that could use a strong powerful six wheel chassis for carrying billets, a large mobile tank for obnoxious or otherwise liquids. The market was there and scrap merchants could earn a few more bob selling on these useful items. Note the Co-operative Wholesale Society (C.W.S) flour mill and grain storage in the background - all since demolished - a reminder of the once wide-ranging industries that flanked the great river. *T.Ermel.*

An artistic shot of the remains of BR Standard 9F 2-10-0 No.92167. Just ten years old when this picture was composed, the 2-10-0 had been withdrawn at Carnforth during the previous June and did not quite make it to 'the end'. Ironically the 9F had, in its past, been allocated to Tyne Dock shed for five months in 1962 but it was sent back to Saltley as surplus to requirements. The low camera angle, combined with the engine silhouetted against a bright white sky, add drama to an otherwise sorry sight. It is now October 1968 and BR steam has been banished for two months or more. The larger numbers of withdrawn steam locomotives are now in decline and the scrapyards will have to look elsewhere for business, although the first generation of British Railways diesel locomotives would soon start to become available but not in the same quantities as the steam motive power. *T.Ermel.*

In November 1965 two Stanier 'Jubilees' turned up at the yard from Leeds Holbeck shed. This is No.45573 NEWFOUNDLAND standing tall and virtually intact between cranes and scrapyard debris - for now. These former LMS engines were amongst the second lot of BR steam locomotives purchased by the company and more were set to follow. The first batch comprised the three Peppercorn A1s secured during June and August 1965. *T.Ermel.*

One for the modellers. Standing behind its tender, also in November 1965, the other Holbeck 'Jubilee' No.45608 GIBRALTAR displays an open view of the cab and drag beam. In the background can be seen a steam crane and on the far side of the river, an ancient naval vessel is moored alongside the Elswick works of Vickers-Armstrong. Both were features of long gone former industries. ***T.Ermel.***

It is 30th January 1966 and the low winter sun highlights the sides of a pair of Gresley V2s, Nos.60876 which was ex York and 60946, a local lad from Gateshead. ***T.Ermel.***

Another former resident of the yard is remembered by this abandoned cab. Gresley V2 No.60886, which arrived from York, was the first engine of the class to receive three separate cylinders and outside steam pipes in 1956. The padded cab seats were reputed to be very comfortable. The rivets and bolts holding the roof of the cab together are well depicted in this 4th March 1967 view. ***T.Ermel.***

This is a late September close-up of the line of engines depicted in our opening view of the Clayton & Davie yard but already, with just a few days having elapsed from that scene, the line-up has changed slightly. Cab to cab now are J27 No.65892 ex Sunderland and Q6 No.63429 ex Tyne Dock, together with an unknown Ivatt 4MT and another Q6. Note in the right background we can see the end aspect of the office building with the port hole window face on. ***T.Ermel.***

More scrapyard jumble in September 1967 with the J27 and Q6 waiting their turn to be broken up ***T.Ermel.***

Ellis Metals Ltd., Swalwell, Derwenthaugh

The Ellis Metals scrapyard was well established by the time that redundant BR steam was being put out to tender. The place had all the rudiments of a 'local' scrap yard with large, heavy metal gates, lots of scrap metal lying around in a seemingly haphazard and dangerous fashion but also a big stripping shed, which would not have looked out of place at a BR locomotive works. That's the way it was in some of the private yards; you entered at your own risk (or peril if large dogs roamed the place) and did not touch anything. Ellis Metals took in just over a couple of dozen ex BR locomotives but some of those were 'class acts' such as the six V2s and a couple of exLMS engines. The others were the everyday 'take them for granted' engines which were quickly missed once they had gone.

ELLIS METALS Scraping List:

LMS Ivatt Cl.4 2-6-0	43075					
LMS Stanier Cl.5 4-6-0	45286					
LNER Gresley V2 2-6-2	60859	60865	60901	60940	60952	60962
LNER Thompson B1 4-6-0	61218	61276	61291			
LNER Q6 0-8-0	63343	63359	63361	63414	63419	63427
LNER J27 0-6-0	65794	65831	65858*	65862		
WD Austeity 8F 2-8-0	90124	90217	90393	90412	90452	90621
BR Standard 9F 2-10-0	92066					

** Did not include the boiler.*

It was widely reported that BR Standard 9F No.92066 had been purchased by George Cohen scrap merchants and hauled to their Cargo Fleet, Middlesbrough yard but that was not the case and the Riddles 2-10-0 ended up inside the Ellis Metals yard at Swalwell, as this 10th August 1965 picture proves. The 9F had been one of the contingent allocated to Tyne Dock shed for working the iron ore trains to Consett and it was the first of them to be withdrawn, which was early by any standards - May 1965. The engine is seen without its tender and has been pushed to the end of a siding waiting for the final moment; it was closely followed by former North Blyth Q6 No.63359, seen in the background. The large gap on the footplate is from where the two Westinghouse air pumps have been removed, the pumps were used for operating the doors on the iron ore hoppers. In the far background can be seen the Ellis Metals sign on the main factory building. *T.Ermel.*

Inside the cutting up shed, on Sunday 17th October 1965, Q6 No.63427 another ex North Blyth engine, is well on its way to oblivion, chunks of scrap metal are littered everywhere. The cutter, no doubt on overtime, is well into the firebox with his oxy-acetylene torch, the prize being all that lovely copper. The sandbox lid retained by a chain can be seen, as well as the severed connecting rod and return crank for operating the mechanical lubricator. Loose asbestos lagging was not considered to be a health hazard in those days. During its forty-five year life, the 0-8-0 had been allocated to just four sheds, three of those - Dairycoates, West Hartlepool, North Blyth - being within sight of the North Sea, the fourth establishment was Consett from where it worked for fourteen years until transferred to North Blyth on 23rd May 1965. That final re-allocation was to prove to be short-lived because on the following 14th June it was condemned. Ellis Metals bought it in the July and arranged for its transit to their yard a few weeks later. ***T.Ermel.***

Another image from 17th October 1965 shows a line up of engines awaiting the cutters torch. They consist a pair of Thompson B1s, Nos.61276 ex York and 61218 formerly of Ardsley, together with WD 2-8-0 No.90124 which was latterly allocated to the last great home of the class - 56A Wakefield. Like some lone sentry, a propane cylinder stands menacingly in the foreground, whilst behind that, a B1 cab (from erstwhile 61291) lies dumped on top of a pile of scrap to remind us of the business carried out at this place. *T.Ermel.*

Another scene from the yard on the 17th October 1965 is this sombre study of a former North Eastern workhorse, J27 No.65794. The 0-6-0 was yet another casualty from North Blyth shed and although still intact, it will not be for much longer. This engine had a bit of a history from BR times. On Saturday 13th October 1956, whilst travelling tender first from Heaton Junction to the shipyards on the Tyne, hauling a train carrying steel plate, it was passing the Avenue branch junction, just north of Monkseaton station when the front axle sheered causing the engine to derail. It then somersaulted and landed on the station platform. Fortunately the only injuries sustained in the incident were a broken arm for the driver and a bout of concussion for the fireman. The wreckage was cleared and traffic was resumed just two days later. Note the acetylene and oxygen cylinders strewn in the foreground. *T.Ermel.*

Two weeks later, on 31st October, all that remains of J27 No.65794 are its two rear coupled wheels and the valuable firebox. It is interesting to note that in some scrapyards the firebox was usually the first thing to be taken (cut/burnt) off a steam locomotive but in the north-east yards that particular gem was seemingly left to the last. In the foreground are a scattering of tender axleboxes probably belonging to this J27. The unceremoniously upturned tender to the left of 65794s firebox had been attached to the WD, No.90124, just a few days before but to enable the recently arrived coaching stock to be accommodated within the yard boundary, the eight-wheel tender was bulldozed off the rails. The carriage standing perilously close to the remains of the J27 reminds us that rolling stock was also another source of sustenance for the cutters at this yard; are those coaches of LMS origin? *T.Ermel.*

W.Willoughby, Choppington station yard, near Morpeth, Northumberland.

When the British Railways goods yard at Choppington, on the Blyth and Tyne system, was closed in March 1964, the site was eventually taken up by Ashington based scrap merchant W.Willoughby so that redundant steam locomotives could arrive straight off BR metals into the newly created but short-lived scrapyard. Virtually on the same line of latitude as the Hughes, Bolckows yard at North Blyth, the Choppington yard was only a few miles away as the crow flies.

It is on record that only twenty-six steam locomotives were cut up at this place, most from local sheds and of North Eastern Railway origin but amongst the list are a few surprises including one Stanier 8F, a Stanier Class 5, and one Fairburn 2-6-4T. Other singletons included a WD, a BR built J72, a Thompson B1 and a Peppercorn K1. Our photographic survey shows mainly Q6 0-8-0s in various states during 1966 and 1967 but the one 'Austerity' taken care of here is also featured for 'balance'. Compared with many private scrapyards operating during the period of 'The Great Cull', Willoughby's was a small operation utilising a convenient location for '...as long as the materials were available...' after which work ceased and the site cleaned up. The passenger services to this place had been withdrawn as long ago as April 1950 but goods trains still run through Choppington. However, the station, associated yard, and all evidence of the scrapping of steam locomotives are long gone.

W.WILLOUGHBY Scrapping List:

ex LMS Fairburn Cl.4P 2-6-4T	42232
ex LMS Stanier Cl.5 4-6-0	44704
ex LMS Stanier Cl.8F 2-8-0	48148
ex LNER Thompson B1 4-6-0	61386
ex LNER Peppercorn K1 2-6-0	62067
ex LNER Q6 0-8-0	63346 63347 63381 63398 63405 63412 63443 63450
ex LNER J27 0-6-0	65795 65817 65832 65833 65835 65838 65841 65842 65862 65865 65872
ex LNER J72 0-6-0T	69006
WD Austerity 8F 2-8-0	90078

The sad remains of Q6 No.63347 in January 1966. Withdrawn at West Hartlepool shed in October 1965, the 0-8-0 has been systematically reduced to half its size. With its boiler tubes ripped out, looking like a disembowelled and very dead dinosaur. Although working for much of its fifty-two year life within the boundaries of the old North Eastern Railway, No.63347 did spend two and a half years away at Doncaster shortly after the Grouping but was back on home territory at Borough gardens shed by the end of June 1928. Sold to Willoughby's in November 1965, the Q6 arrived here at the temporary scrapyard the following month. *I.Spencer.*

Seen from the opposite of the 'main line,' a half eaten away Q6, No.63450. This was another former West Hartlepool based engine which had been condemned in December 1966, purchased by Willoughby's in February 1967 and by the following May was on its way to oblivion. What a mess! ***E.Wilson.***

From a different but no less stressful angle, No.63450 presents its innards to all and sundry. With a cut away smokebox and boiler cladding, exposing superheater elements, snifting valve and boiler tubes, this is indeed an undignified fate for the Q6. Note the ex narrow gauge mining tub alongside the 0-8-0. With colliery closures, contractions and modernisation all taking place during this period, the local NCB installations were another good source of scrap metal. *E.Wilson.*

About as bad as it gets for a steam locomotive before its ceases to exist. It is March 1967 and this is the firebox and rear axle which form the partial remains of Q6 No.63381, another engine from south of the Tyne. Resident at Tyne Dock from January 1966 to withdrawal in December, the Q6 was purchased for scrap in February 1967 and as can be gathered it soon got here. This illustration is a good guide for a live steam modeller as it shows the position of the tubes and boiler stays albeit on a grander scale. I wonder if the cutter has retired to the Railway Tavern for refreshments? This area of Choppington was called Willow Bridge but that obviously had no railway connection because the road crossed the railway on the level here by the erstwhile station. *E.Wilson.*

This was the smokebox saddle of No.63381, showing the blastpipe and steampipes leading to the cylinders. This is yet another educating but sad perspective for the uninitiated of how a steam locomotive works. Note the proximity of the main line in the background. *E.Wilson.*

Here is a nice change for the better, albeit a brief one in July 1967. This lone 'Austerity' No.90078 is a recent addition to the dwindling Choppington allocation and came from Sunderland. With its cylinder end cover missing, we can probably guess the reason for its very recent withdrawal. Note the small BR containers to the left of the 8F. These would have been bought as scrap 'for a song' and were ideal for equipment storage during the short period that Willoughby's operated this site. ***E.Wilson.***

Lets finish off the Willoughby section with a view of this fairly intact but nevertheless windowless Q6 as photographed in May 1967. This is No.63412, ex West Hartlepool, and now without a smokebox door, however, it does enable us to view details of the inside, especially one of the curving steam pipes. ***E.Wilson.***

Hughes, Bolckows Ltd.

Battleship Wharf, North Blyth, Northumberland

Latecomers into the railway locomotive scrapping business, Hughes, Bolckow did not drag their heels once they had started and were soon making up for any lost time. Their proximity to the engine sheds at North Blyth was useful, especially during the latter days of NE Region steam. However, the yard did take in some of the former 'glamour boys' in the shape of ex LNER Pacifics. More interesting, perhaps, were the former LMS 'namers' which journeyed from the west coast to join some of the lesser types. Below is a list of engines known to have been cut up at the yard and although this in itself should not be regarded as a complete portfolio, it is fairly comprehensive and accurate. Most of the engines scrapped here came from nearby sheds such as Sunderland, Tyne Dock and West Hartlepool but others travelled far such as BR Standard No.75060 which was brought from Croes Newydd. It cost the yard £1,865 to purchase and its 82 tons arrived on 14th September 1967.

HUGHES BOLCKLOW Scrapping List:

LMS Fowler Cl.4 2-6-4T	42405	42414								
LMS 4F 0-6-0	43908									
LMS Stanier 'Jubilee' 6P & 7P 4-6-0	45584	45736								
LMS 3F 0-6-0T	47230	47345								
LNER Gresley A4 4-6-2	60001	60024	60026	60034						
LNER Gresley A3 4-6-2	60040	60051	60083	60084						
LNER Peppercorn A1 4-6-2	60114	60116	60127	60132	60142	60158				
LNER Thompson B1 4-6-0	61012	61014	61016	61021	61023	61037	61070	61107	61110	61127
	61162	61167								
	61188	61220	61238	61248	61257	61259	61275	61304	61313	61320
	61353	61367								
	61385	61387	61388	61394						
LNER B16 4-6-0	61421	61434	61448	61454	61457					
LNER Peppercorn K1 2-6-0	62002	62003	62004	62006	62007	62008	62010	62011	62017	62022
	62024	62030								
	62037	62045	62046	62049	62050	62054	62055	62059	62060	62062
LNER Q6 0-8-0	63349	63360	63362	63363	63371	63379	63386	63389	63394	63401
	63406	63410								
	63421	63431	63435	63436	63437	63445	63446	63454		
LNER J37 0-6-0	64595									
LNER J27 0-6-0	65788	65789	65790	65796	65801	65802	65804	65805	65808	65812
	65813	65814								
	65819	65821	65822	65823	65825	65834	65844	65846	65851	65853
	65859	65860								
	65861	65869	65870	65874	65878	65880	65885	65893		
LNER Gresley V1 2-6-2T	67642	67651								
LNER 'WD' J94 0-6-0ST	68014	68019								
BR Standard Cl.4 4-6-0	75060									
BR Standard Cl.2MT 2-6-2T	84001	84011	84018	84020						
WD Austerity 8F 2-8-0	90009	90135	90348	90378	90382	90417	90478	90627	90677	90695
BR Standard Cl.9F 2-10-0	92062	92179	92221							

You can almost feel the biting wind coming off the North Sea and straight onto the back of the photographer as he lined up his camera to capture this panoramic view of Hughes, Bolckows yard in January 1965. Taken from the footbridge which spanned the line to the coal staiths, just south of the site, and North Blyth engine shed, the view reveals much of interest which is now mainly history. The line of rolling stock in the open ground is formed of withdrawn North Tyneside electric units. Just above the first coach on the right, A4 No.60001 SIR RONALD MATTHEWS can be seen in the yard's cutting area with numerous ex BR and NCB mineral wagons tossed about like toys. The yard fronts onto the river by the tidal basin and whenever ships arrived alongside, it was always done to coincide with a high tide so that the vessels were then grounded at low tide. The address of the yard gives a clue as to its main purpose and many warships have met their end at this place. Across the River Blyth, on the south bank can be seen the old colliery headgear dwarfed by the large new headgear at Bates Colliery. A collier is alongside the Bates 'Pit' wharf but Britain was not exporting much coal at this time so it must have been a coastal vessel headed for the Thames, a traditional destination for Northumberland coal throughout the Twentieth century. This industrial scene has now vanished and been replaced with a new facility to receive coal from Romania and South America and wherever else the UK gets its coal from. *I.Spencer.*

Gresley A4 Pacific No.60001 SIR RONALD MATTHEWS, the first locomotive in the Ian Allan Eastern Region ABC, on a cold and snowswept January day in 1965. Masquerading now as a 2-6-2, the once proud locomotive would soon be reduced to small chunks of metal of the size to fit inside the charging cars of the blast furnaces. Withdrawn three months before this scene was captured on film, and a Gateshead engine for the whole of its life, the external condition of the engine, even in these surroundings, is quite admirable for a 52A Pacific. Besides the locomotive only ever having one shed, No.60001 also only ever had one tender, No.5674 but that is nowhere to be seen and might possibly have been cut up already because the locomotive had been at the yard for about a month. ***W.P.Hodgson.***

Overlooked by the vulture-like presence of the scrapyard cranes, the depressing sight of a group of North Tyneside electric units waiting for the cutters torch. The bucket style seats within these units were very comfortable and no doubt one or two ended in different corners of the yard for further use. The letters 'COND', short for condemned on the unit's side, were used frequently on coaches and wagons. This particular coach is E29235E as it was in January 1965. ***W.P.Hodgson.***

A somewhat brighter and warmer day during that January of 1965 provides us with an alternate view of No.60001. Displaying the open 'cods mouth', we get a chance to see the double chimney courtesy of the missing casing. The double chimney was a late addition to the A4, being fitted during a General overhaul in April 1958. The nameplate on this side appears to have been burnt off, no doubt at either Gateshead or Heaton. The front pair of bogie wheels had been removed to enable the engine to negotiate the tightly curved crossing into the scrap yard. All the Pacifics which entered this yard required the same treatment, due to their substantial length. *W.P.Hodgson.*

It was perhaps inevitable that the former LMS Fowler 2-6-4 tanks allocated to Darlington shed should end up in a north-east scrapyard. This is No.42405 awaiting its fate in the white light of an icy cold 4th January 1965. One of a pair of its kind which were scrapped here along with five other former LMS types. *I.Spencer.*

Later that year, on Thursday 5th August, this general view of part of the yard reveals two Peppercorn Pacifics Nos.60142 EDWARD FLETCHER and 60116 HAL O' THE WYND, albeit without nameplates but otherwise intact and with front bogies yet to be chopped in half. Both of these A1s were formerly allocated at Gateshead shed but arrived at Bolckow's yard ex store from Tyne Dock shed after months of redundancy - their external condition is more like the normal Gateshead presentation we got used to. The weeds and scrapyard debris surround the engines but they will soon be taken inside the yard where the business of dismantling these Pacifics in the crudest way possible would take place. Meanwhile the other business of Blyth carried on unceasingly as witnessed by the rows of laden 21T coal hoppers lined up in the background waiting to discharge their load into the waiting ships. For the record Al Nos. 60127 and 60132 were the third and fourth members of the A1 gang which arrived at the yard during the last week of July and first week of August 1965 – the Hughes, Bulckow works holiday. *I.Spencer.*

On the same day we get a broadside view of No.60116. This engine spent its last ten years allocated variously to Heaton, Tweedmouth or Gateshead depots. The scrap value of an A1 in the summer of 1965 was £3000, a figure in stark contrast with the cost of the privately built and recently completed Al No.60163 TORNADO which has cost £3,000,000! No doubt about it, a great opportunity was missed when all the Peppercorn engines were allowed to be scrapped whilst numerous A4s were preserved one way or another. Now as for the WD 2-8-0s, I could go on and on about that particular omission because .... *I.Spencer.*

As seen from over the fence in Bolckow's yard, Gresley A3 Pacific No.60051 BLINK BONNY waiting beneath the hovering yard cranes for its turn with the cutting crew in February 1965. The engine appears to be coupled to an A1 tender which surely must have been coupled on at Heaton for the journey to North Blyth. In its working life, this coupling would not have been possible, as the A3s did not have steam brakes on the locomotives and tenders, whereas the Peppercorn A1s were equipped with them. Although not best placed to view the whole of this locomotive, the Witte type smoke deflectors fitted to these engines in their latter years certainly gave them a new and arguably better look. *I.Spencer.*

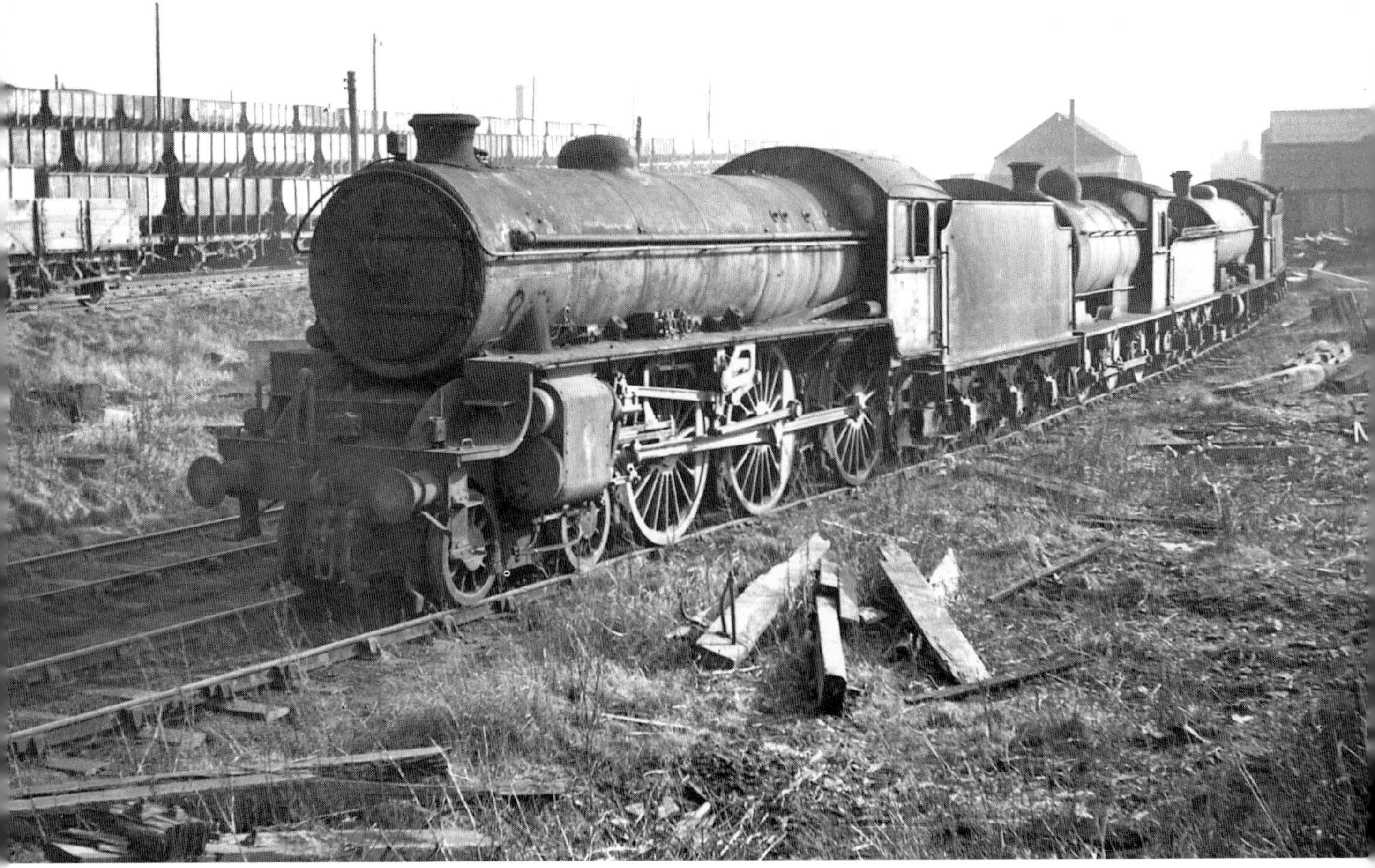

Back into the open ground between the yard and the staiths - the storage area. It is now April 1966 and the chances of seeing 'namers' at this place is becoming rarer. However, this Thompson B1, No.61248 (honest) once carried the name GEOFFREY GIBBS but that was obviously some time in the past and the wearing of nameplates by now was very rare - operational or not. A long way from its former home at Colwick shed, the B1 has joined the queue to enter the yard and is in the company of a J27 and a Q6. In the middle background can be seen the gradients of the lines approaching the coal staiths and although the wagons are still the same as in previous years, the motive power which pushed them up the inclines had by now become diesel shunters which although highly efficient and one man operated, did not have the same effect on observers watching an ex NER 0-6-0T hammering along at full throttle and making a noise which could perhaps be heard miles away. *I.Spencer.*

WD 2-8-0 No.90009, formerly of Sunderland South Dock shed, has been brought to the yard in November 1967. By now steam on the North Eastern Region has finished and this engine was amongst the last of them working right to the end. Sunderland shed had housed ex NER 0-8-0 and 0-6-0 tender engines for much of its existence but during its latter years it became home for a large number of these 'Austerity' 2-8-0s which had been made redundant at depots such as Wakefield or Hull Dairycoates. Note that its motion was probably stored in the coal space of the tender for the short transit to its impending doom. ***E.Wilson.***

Under a laden sky in January 1965 W.P.Hodgson captured this fine study of Stanier 'Jubilee' No.45584 NORTH WEST FRONTIER, which was ex store at Carlisle Kingmoor shed. One of two 'Jubs' dispatched at Bolckows, this engine had been condemned in September 1964 after a turbulent eighteen months which saw it undertake five different transfers from Blackpool to Saltley, then Willesden to Preston and finally Kingmoor. One of the North British built examples from 1934, the 4-6-0 had at least fulfilled its theoretical thirty years useful and economical life. Buffered up to the 6P is 'Jinty' No.47345, which was another September 1964 withdrawal from Kingmoor. After spending much of the 1950s at Longsight, it transferred to Barrow in November 1959 and spent its last two years at Carlisle. Many of the movements of condemned locomotives from their place of storage to their eventual place of demise usually took place at night but there was so many of these movements to private scrapyards during the latter years that it was not always possible for BR to hide its skeletons under cover of darkness and inevitably they sometimes had to travel by day. Nevertheless, pictures of engines in transit to scrapyards are fairly rare except perhaps those taken on the Southern Region during the mass movements to the South Wales yards. ***W.P.Hodgson.***

Later during that month of January 1965 another 'Jubilee' turned up from Kingmoor and again a 'Jinty was included in the consignment for good measure -No.47230. Nose to nose with No.47345, rebuilt 'Jubilee' No.45736 PHOENIX was certainly not going to rise from the ashes after its arrival here. For all intents and purposes No.45736, along with No.45735 COMET, was a rebuilt 'Scot' and had the same Diagram 2A boiler with double chimney and was classified 7P. Rebuilt during 1942, the 4-6-0 spent much of its life thereafter working from Crewe North shed but ended up at Kingmoor in September 1964 only to be condemned on arrival from nearby Upperby. The year of 1964 saw no less than 66 'Jubilees' withdrawn, virtually half the class. There was no sign of the ex Midland 0-6-0T No.47230 but it had, until March 1957, been resident in South Wales for much of its life at the Midland's own depot at Upper Bank near Swansea but transferred north to Bank Hall in Liverpool prior to a stint in Manchester at both Agecroft and Newton Heath. Finally Carlisle Kingmoor got it and from there to here! *I.Spencer.*

The mangled mess of the valve gear and slide bars of Peppercorn K1 No.62059 at North Blyth shed in February 1967. Deemed uneconomical to repair, the 2-6-0 was condemned on Sunday 12th February 1967 and waited at that shed until eventually purchased by Bolckows in late April. Once the deal was secured, the K1 was dragged across the road to the scrap yard for cutting up. Ten years previously this engine would have been taken to main works and given a thorough repair, not just because of its then youth but because it would have been economical to do so; by February 1967 however, it was a death sentence. *F. Wilson.*

Besides scrapping railway locomotives, warships, and all manner of industrial machinery, Hughes, Bolckow also took in road vehicles, especially former municipal bus fleets such as this gaggle of condemned AEC-built Newcastle Corporation buses. They appear to be huddled together for warmth on a cold January day in 1967. Note that they have been robbed of their destination boards and radiator badges. The tyres do not look too promising either and some would be dubiously 'bald' by today's standards; perhaps the decent ones had been swapped. Their consecutive registration numbers, matching their fleet numbers, give clues as to their origin: 256, 258, 260, 261. *E.Wilson.*

Gresley A4 Pacific No.60024 KINGFISHER, a long time resident and favourite of Edinburgh's Haymarket shed, was transferred to Aberdeen Ferryhill to work on the Glasgow—Aberdeen 3-hour expresses. Originally fitted with a corridor tender (No.5331 to February 1957 then No.5329 to 24th August 1966) for hauling Edinburgh—Kings Cross trains, it stands in its final form, fitted with a streamlined non-corridor tender (No.5640) and sadly bereft of its nameplates. The backing plate from the Kingfisher crest can still be seen on the boiler side. Condemned in September 1966, the A4 was sold to H,B the following month but it did not arrive in Blyth until January 1967. Study of its body side reveals evidence of a struggle to remove the nameplate on this side - hopefully the plate was not too badly damaged! ***E.Wilson.***